FUN ONLINE GAMES FOR TEENS WITH TIPS AND TRICKS: Ages 13 And Up

Speedy Publishing LLC
40 E. Main St. #1156
Newark, DE 19711
www.speedypublishing.com

Massively multiplayer online role-playing games (MMORPGs) blend the genres of role-playing video games and massively multiplayer online games, potentially in the form of web browser-based games, in which a very large number of players interact with one another within a world.

ArcheAge

is an MMORPG developed by Korean developer Jake Song (former developer of Lineage) and his development company, XL Games. The game was released in Korea on January 15, 2013, Europe and North America on September 16, 2014, and has also had a closed beta in China. ArcheAge is described as a "sandpark" MMORPG, which the developers say is a hybrid of the open content style of a "sandbox" game and the more structured play experience of a "themepark" game.

Tips and Tricks

Leveling

If you have patron, time your crafting, trade runs, and irl chores like food and hygiene breaks with the state of PvP in your leveling zone. At level 30+, anyone can PvP you at any time provided you are not in the few safe spots on the map. Open up your map and constantly check the status of conflict in your current questing zone. If it says "WAR ENDS IN 30 MINUTES", then after those 30 minutes you will have 1-4 hours of peace time where no one can distract you while you quest. PvP is fun, but not level 50s are stomping your level 30 zone. Peace time is a way to level through the griefers.

Save your purses for maximum efficiency. As I mentioned earlier, labor consumption = exp. This scales with your level. The longer you wait to consume labor to open purses, the more experience you will obtain from them.

Farming

Claiming land on a slope provides you with more surface area allowing you to retrieve more fruitful harvests (e.g., there are claims to grow 24 trees on a sloped 16x16 instead of the 20 cap on flat land).

Each zone is flagged as Arid, Tropical, Temperate, or Subarctic. Highlight a seed or sapling to see which climate it thrives in, and prioritize these. (e.g., Traveler's Tree > Aspen Tree if you have land in a Tropical climate).

Things to do at certain thresholds

Level 10

Choose your last skillset and get your class.

Level 20

Max out your glider

Level 30

Become a juror by talking to any honor point quest collector to begin the quest chain.

Note: Must have 0 infamy and crime points (two daily quests to remove 30 of each; Rookborne and Sanddeep

Level 40

If you have completed 5 trials as a juror, you can begin the Bounty Hunter quest chain from an honor point guard. This quest gives you a cloak with +7 to all stats.

RuneScape

is a fantasy massively multiplayer online role-playing game (MMORPG) released in January 2001 by Andrew and Paul Gower, and developed and published by Jagex Games Studio. It is a graphical browser game implemented on the client-side in Java or HTML5, and incorporates 3D rendering. The game has had over 200 million accounts created and is recognised by the Guinness World Records as the world's largest free MMORPG and the most-updated game.

Tips and Tricks

Money

If you are looking for a quick pile of cash and don't know where to go; all new players can earn a quick stack of cash by completing the Stronghold of Player Safety. Players can also complete the tasks in the achievement system for a sizable amount of starting money, but this will require a deal of effort and time.

Skill

Skills are the heart of RuneScape. Free players have access to 16 skills, while members have access to all 25 skills. Skill levels are gained when enough experience is gained in that skill. In turn, experience is gained by practising a skill or doing quests. The higher your level, the more things you can do that are related to that skill.

Questing

Another favourite pastime in RuneScape are Quests. All quest starting locations can be identified by the quest symbol Quest map icon. Quests are a group of interrelated tasks. There are short ones and long ones, but here are a few that are recommended to new players. Most Quests give some reward, such as coins, experience, items, or access to places and certain skills. Quests are usually started by talking to a certain NPC. You can find who that someone is by clicking on the quest name in the quest list, found on the right of the screen.

Combat

Combat with high level monsters is amongst the best sources of profit in the game. Every player must start small, which means if you want to be killing mighty dragons, you must start with cows.

Combat in RuneScape is very unique. There are three styles, Magic, Melee, and Ranged. These are at opposing points in the "Combat Triangle". Ranged is strong against Magic, Magic is strong against Melee, and Melee is strong against Ranged.

Tasks

Tasks are a good source of starting money while getting you involved in the various aspects of the game. When starting out, only low level tasks will be available, however as skill level up more tasks will be accessible. Rewards can be claimed from Explorer Jack in Lumbridge, and you can easily earn 10,000 coins in a short amount of time.

Death

Upon death, you will keep three of your most valuable items (with certain exceptions), and a gravestone will fall on the location of your death, safe keeping your items for a certain amount of time (which varies with the type of gravestone).

Once your character dies you are teleported to the NPC Death. You will be able to recover your items for a price based on how much your equipment costs.

To upgrade gravestones, players must complete the Restless Ghost quest.

World of Tanks

is a massively multiplayer online game developed by Belarusian-Cypriot[3] company Wargaming, featuring early to mid-20th century era fighting vehicles.[4] It is built upon a freemium business model where the game is free-to-play, but participants also have the option of paying a fee for use of "premium" features. The focus is on player vs. player gameplay with each player controlling an armored vehicle, which may be a Light, Medium or Heavy tank, tank destroyer, or self-propelled gun. World of Tanks debuted as an eSports game at

Tips and Tricks

How to choose a tank

Unsurprisingly, Maxfield says that terrain is key. "You have city maps and you have open maps and you have hybrid maps which are a mixture. You choose a tank based on that. There are light tanks like the AMX 13 90 which is a lot faster and smaller, but it doesn't have as much firepower, armour or as much HP [as other tanks]. On an open map where you need to get from A to B quickly you want something smaller, faster, lighter. On city maps you want something heavy because you don't have to travel as far and when you're driving down a street you can only get shot from the front so you need more armour on the front. A lot of people pick tanks from the country they come from. When you're a newcomer the British are pretty good and the Americans are pretty good."

But if in doubt...

Just go for a tank you've heard of and which looks the coolest!

Always be thinking of your next move

"You're moving from cover to cover, from A to B and you're always thinking about what's at B. You don't want to get there and be like 'Well... I'm in the middle of a field'. The average battle time is seven and a half minutes so that's seven and a half minutes thinking about your next step," explains Maxfield. "The worst people at World of Tanks are the best people at Counter-Strike even though they seem like very similar games because they're impatient. You have to be a little patient to play the game."

Don't be that lone tanker

"Always think about your team," Maxfield says. "You should never be in a situation where you're unsupported no matter how good a player you are. You should always have someone with line of sight on you. That's the most important thing for beginners, otherwise they just drive into the middle of nowhere and get themselves destroyed. That's what I did!"

Taking one for the team

"The more guns in the game, the more likely you are to win," says Maxfield. "If you lose a player you can lose a lot more easily. Even if you have to lose some HP drive in front of your mate [when they're in danger]. If he doesn't die and you lose 300 HP so be it. He's still alive – he can help you and still shoot. So that's very important, blocking for your team-mates.

And finally...

Where you're hit matters just as much as whether you're hit at all. "Always have your tracks showing rather than the superstructure of the tank because tracks don't take any damage," says Maxfield. "Also angle your armour as much as possible. If your armour is angled they're less likely to be able to penetrate your tank."

"Angling your tank properly can significantly increase the chance of an opponent's shell bouncing off your armour," Passemard adds. "If done properly, just angling your hull can be the decisive factor between a loss or win in a one-on-one duel or even a game."

MU ONLINE

was created in December 2001 by the Korean gaming company Webzen. Like most MMORPGs, players have to create a character among seven different classes and to set their foot on the MU Continent. In order to gain experience and thus to level up, a players needs to fight monsters (mobs). MU is populated by a large variety of monsters, from simple ones like goblins and golems, to frightening ones such as the Gorgon, Kundun or Selupan. Each monster-type is unique, has different spawn points, and drops different items.

Tips and Tricks

Bonus character

Select any normal character class and get to level 220 to unlock the Magic Gladiator at the character selection screen.

Easy money

Go to Lorencia. Go to the blacksmith and buy the first gold weapon and sell it. It will be sold for a higher price than it was bought.

Safe spots in Davias

Outside the town of Davias, there are some safe spots. when entering these spots, you cannot attack or being attacked. It works as if you entering a town.
The coordination of these spots are:
169,25
171,25
172,25
173,24
199,178
209,178

Emotes

Enter one of the following case-sensitive messages to perform the corresponding emote.

No gesture: /Don't or /Never
Arm pump: /OK
Beckon someone: /Come
Bow: /Hello or /Thanks
Clap: /Good, /Nice, or /Wow
Cross arms: /-_-
Head scratch: /; or /Sorry
Kneel: /Respect
Laugh: /^^ or /Haha
Lead your men forward: /Rush
Points to where you are facing: /That
Raise both arms: /beat it or /Great
Rub arms: /Cold or /hurts
Sadness: /Sad
Salute: /Sir
Cry: /Cry or /T_T or /Sad
Victory pose : /Victory or /Win
Wave: /Bye

RAGNARÖK ONLINE

is a Korean massive multiplayer online role-playing game or MMORPG created by GRAVITY Co., Ltd. based on the manhwa Ragnarok by Lee Myung-jin. It was first released in South Korea on 31 August 2002 for Microsoft Windows and has since been released in many other locales around the world. The game has spawned an animated series, Ragnarok the Animation, and a sequel game, Ragnarok Online 2: Legend of the Second. Player characters exist in a world with a player environment that gradually changes with the passage of time.

Tips and Tricks

How to get easy zeny

Go to anthell F1 and keep killing the vivata ants (fat ones,purple); while collecting both their royal jelly and hney pots (dont use them).Then,go to any towns and sell all of them.!!!!!YOU GET A LOT OF ZENY!

Continuous attack

Type /noctrl in the whispering box and then your character attacks continuously until the creature dies. (note: not applicable to magic spells)

Easy Stun

Be a Swordman, and get Bash at level 10. Get Fatal Blow. Get a blade with 4 slot and insert 4 Savage Babe card. Use Bash on a monster and it will normally get stunned.

Easy experience

Find a monster that will heal itself, such as the Smokie (Racoon). Hit it a few times and let it heal itself. Depending on how much it healed itself, your experience should increase. You can get about three times the normal experience from the monster when doing this.

Enter one of the following commands in the chat window to activate the feature.

Result	Code
Open today's tips	- /tip
Show other control keys	- /h (help)
Show number of players on same server	- /w (who)
Show current location	- /where
Auto attack enemies without [Ctrl] + click	- /nc
Continue attacks; does not work on spells.	- /noctrl
Auto heal enemies (undead) without holding [Shift]	- /ns
Lists blocked personal messages	- /ex
Block personal messages from named players	- /ex [character name]
Allow personal messages from named players	- /in [character name]
Allow personal messages from everyone	- /inall
Block personal messages from everyone	- /exall
Leave current party	- /leave
Kick player from your created party	- /expel [character name]
Save current chat dialogue	- /savechat
Turn camera focus on	- /camera On
Turn camera focus off	- /camera Off
Save warp point; only with Warp Portal skill	- /memo
Toggle fog effects	- /fog
Create a party	- /organize [party name]
Create a Guild; must have Emperium item	- /guild [guild name]
Disband Guild that you created	- /gocp [guild name]
Toggle skill and casting effects	- /effect
Toggle red miss indicator	- /miss

GunBound

is a free-to-play, turn-based, room-to-room, multiplayer online game with many similar features to the popular Worms game series.

GunBound was developed and is maintained by South Korean developer Softnyx. It is currently in its third major release, subtitled Season 2 internationally. It was called GunBound Revolution in North America with ijji as its host before it was shut down on July 24, 2009. The first major beta release was Thor's Hammer.

Tips and Tricks

Dragon and Knight

Use the following trick to get the hidden mobiles, Dragon and Knight. Pick "Random" and you have a 1:16 chance of getting one of those mobiles.

Secret Mobiles

There are two Secret Mobiles that aren't seen in the Mobile Select Screen. They are very powerful, so you only get them if you select Random as your mobile. You have a 1/18 of getting one of these.

Never Get Kicked Out

Just simply name yourself a swear or unpolite word. You can do this by changing your name (which costs money) or you can name yourself this in the first place.Whoever tries to kick you out, it will just say: "Please do not use impolite words."

For limitless avatar

send 5,000 gold to laxnick and type code [the sheep are in the barn] then he will automatically activate the cheat and give any of your avatars that you are currently holding a limitless supply.

Grub SS

sometime, grub's ss doesn't make a big damage, but actually it can makes a REALLY BIG damage. in a place, you must go near to the enemy the make a small hole and don't let them go. then you must fire the ss direct to the hole (don't make the ball go) then it can make 800 damage.

Ready but the Master don't see

Reason: Suddenly this bug occur in network problem...but dont worry there is a solution on that and its easy and simple.

Solution: When you're ready but the Master don't see. you should rejoin or go to other rooms.

CABAL ONLINE

is a free-to-play, 3D massively multiplayer online role-playing game developed by South Korean company ESTsoft. Different localizations of the game exist for various countries and regions. Although free-to-play, the game makes use of the freemium business model by implementing an "Item Shop", both in-game and via web, allowing players to purchase special premium coins using real currency, in order to acquire exclusive game enhancements and features, useful items and assorted vanity content.

Tips and Tricks

Easy money

To gain almost double alz drop go to npcs and buy LUCK equipment (example: Armaid Martialsuit of Luck).

Easier quests

Some quests usually involve killing the same thing. Rather than doing them one by one, do these quests all at the same time. For example, you may get a quest that involves killing several skeletons, skeleton warriors, and skeleton mages. Because they are all in the same area, stack all these quests at the same time and then do them together to save valuable time.

Easy skills

When you are about level 50 to 60 go to traders and buy Adept equipment. The Adept Suit will give you +Skill Exp. Once you have full Adept equipment (suit, weapons, rings, and amulets) go to Port Lux to Instructor and buy Change Force Skill (upgrade), Change Force Sword if you want to make sword experience (you must use magic to easy level up the sword experience), and Change Force Magic if you want to make magic experience (you must use sword to easy level up magic experience).

Easy skill experience

When you are around level 50-60 go to traders and buy "adept" equipment. The adept suit will give you +skill exp.Once you have full adept equipment (suit,weapons,rings and amulets)go in Port Lux to Instructor and buy CHANGE FORCE Skill (upgrade),CF Sword if you want to make sword xp (you must use magic to easy skill up the sword exp),CF Magic if you want to make magic xp (you must use sword to easy skill up magic)

Unequip all your weapons and find an area where you can "Punch" (normal attack) an orange-named (strong level) monster for 1 point of damage. Although 1 point of damage is best, doing 2 to 10 points is fine, but you will gain less skill experience. Click the monster, press [Normal Attack], and your character should start attacking the monster constantly, without you having to do anything except change to another target once the previous one dies. If you must use skills like Regeneration to keep healing, it is recommended you get a "Life Absorb Ring", which will constantly absorb HP from the damage you deal to a monster. To make this even easier and require less attention, play the game in windowed mode.

FLYFF

(SHORT FOR FLY FOR FUN)

is a fantasy MMORPG by Korean development company Gala Lab (formerly Aeonsoft & nFlavor).[1] Flyff is a fairly typical party-oriented grinding game where no character can do everything; efficient play requires working in groups to level up by killing monsters, or Masquerpets. Its main distinctiveness lies in its flying system: flying is the normal method of transportation for characters above level 20.

Tips and Tricks

Easy Penya, items, and experience

Talk to Paul in the first city. He will ask you to get twenty wings. Kill twenty bat creatures and you will gain experience for the kills, their items, and Penya. You will also get 100 Penya after you talk to Paul.

Double jump

The following double jump trick can end up as a higher jump depending on how many enemies you have. First get an enemy that cannot kill you, like the Aibat. Make the monster follow you. You must be running or walking (recommended). When the monster screeches, jump. The monster will attack you in the air and you will jump a second time. This can be used to get up in trees and on tall houses.

Jumping Very high Without Scroll of Velocity

You Must Have Many Monsters Attacking you (But not high lvls) do not use any weapons just your hand after mobbing try running and jumping on the misses and you will jump so high! When not Try doing it again, its very Fun Go try it!

No Walking

* Jump in the air.
* While in the air hold forwards and right or forwards and left.
* When u land ur char will start to move in a circle without feet moving.
* Keep holding forward and wat ever either left or right (which ever your choice was).
* Press the other button while still holding the others down to turn the otherway.

Hint

In flyff if you have a transform (ex lawolf trans) and a no disguise, you can go through the mas mine and go to the end without being attacked by those pesky angry giants.

RF ONLINE

is a 3D MMORPG developed by CCR. The first version of the game was released in South Korea and was later followed by Chinese (Mandarin), Japanese, Indonesia, Portuguese and English translations. The North American/European version of the game launched its retail phase on February 21, 2006. A mixture of science fiction and classic fantasy, RF Online is set in a distant planet in the Novus system where magic exists alongside high technology. Like most MMORPGs it follows the typical fantasy setting complete with swords and sorcery, but it also emphasizes the three-way Race vs. Race vs. Race (RvRvR) concept and modern/futuristic technology such as mecha and nuclear weapons.

Tips and Tricks

Easy experience

Use the following tricks for easy early leveling with shield and knife (levels close range, shield, and defense).

Warrior: Intense shield and knife creates intense defense with a decent attack.

Spiritualist: Having a Spirit knife that increases FP recovery by 500% and will help you maintain a spell fiesta without many potions. A shield could benefit if you are dependent on not dying.

Ranger: When the Long Range skill is maxed, use this combo to stay powerful and alive. Defense is not given much to a ranger. Leveling close range can be difficult. Intense works well.

Specialist: Intense shield and knife really protects the health they lack. Long range weapons will be useful if they prefer avoiding damage altogether.

EVE Online

is a player-driven, persistent-world massively multiplayer online role-playing game (MMORPG) set in a science fiction space setting, developed and published by CCP Games. Characters pilot customizable ships through a galaxy of 7,800 star systems.[2][3] Most star systems are connected to one or more other star systems by means of stargates. The star systems can contain moons, planets, stations, wormholes, asteroid belts and complexes.

Tips and Tricks

Don't play the game in AFK mode. This game is not designed with this kind of playing style in mind and you should NEVER consider your ship and character safe while being away from your computer.

Don't expect CONCORD to keep you immune to attacks or ship losses. Like in the real world, law enforcement often arrives too late at the scene of the crime, even though they able to punish the criminal, they can't always prevent the crime.

Don't rely on Sentry Guns to keep you a 100% safe. Especially not when traveling in unsecured space. There are several tactical ways to avoid sentry gun fire, which are NOT considered to be an exploit.

Use map filters such as "ships destroyed in the last hour" to spot possible player pirate camps and other dangerous areas.

Use the local chat channel to see what's happening within the system when you have just jumped in. If people warp jam your ship, offer to pay them to stay alive - sometimes it works and any chance is better than the alternative.

Use Warp Core Stabilizers to avoid being warp jammed. The more, the merrier. When you are warp scrambled you are not dead yet. You can still escape by moving away from the spot if they didn't web you. For this, double click on empty space.

Use the overview scanner and set it to alert you when anyone in scanning range is a potential threat to you.

Even in low security space, some stations have sentry guns, so if things get desperate its better to retreat to a station with sentry guns than a Jump Gate that doesn't have any.

The safest locations in low security space are in the middle of nowhere. If all gates are being monitored and there are no Stations with Sentry guns to retreat to, bookmark a few locations while in warp, and then warp back to one of your bookmarks. Sit it out there but be ready to warp to another of the bookmarks if anyone finds you.

When cloaked and stationary at a hostile gate, hit MWD (microwarp drive) set to manual for a 10 second burn; by the time you come uncloaked and hit your destination, the last bit of MWD will spin you around and get you into warp a lot faster.

MapleStory

is a free-to-play, 2D, side-scrolling massively multiplayer online role-playing game, developed by the South Korean company Wizet.

In the game, players travel the "Maple World", defeating monsters and developing their characters' skills and abilities as is typical in role-playing games. Players can interact with others in many ways, such as through chatting, trading and playing minigames. Groups of players can band together in parties to hunt monsters and share the rewards and can also collaborate forming guilds to interact more easily with each other.

MAPLE STORY FIFTH ANNIVERSARY
5th

Tips and Tricks

Easy money

If you are level 35 or higher, hunt Sakura Cellions on Amoria: Purple Plains, which give about 232 to 348 Mesos per kill. They are level 33 and have 1100 HP. They drop Cellion Tails which are exchange quest items and sell for quite a bit. They also drop level 50 equips such as the Thief Red China Set (male), level 50 warrior helm that can be sold for quite a bit, if its over average on STR; and the Red Anakamoon Level 58 magician overall and cape for STR 100%. They do not do much damage. You can get more than 300,000 Mesos an hour by doing this.

Note: Many people go there and might "kill steal" you.

Easy experience

For levels 1 to 5, stay at the Maple camp. From levels 5 to-8, train on Snails and do missions. From 8 to 14 fight red Snails, Stumps and Slimes. From levels 14 to 20 fight Pigs, Ribbon Pigs, Orange Mushrooms, and Green Mushrooms. For faster levels, just focus on Green Mushrooms. From levels 20 to 30 fight in Ant Tunnels 1 and 2 or do party quests in Kerning. For faster levels just focus on Ant Tunnels.

Easy experience for spellcasters

Go to Ellinia and buy some potions. Then find and fight some slimes and snails (tree stump is not that effective). Fight until your life, mana, and potions run out. You should have enough money to buy more potions. Do so, restore yourself, and fight again. For levels 1 to 5, stay at the Maple camp. From levels 5 to-8, train on Snails and do missions. From 8 to 14 fight red Snails, Stumps and Slimes. From levels 14 to 20 fight Pigs, Ribbon Pigs, Orange Mushrooms, and Green Mushrooms. For faster levels, just focus on Green Mushrooms. From levels 20 to 30 fight in Ant Tunnels 1 and 2 or do party quests in Kerning. For faster levels just focus on Ant Tunnels.

Extra Mesos

Drop about 10 Mesos. It will become 15 Mesos when picked up.

As in all RPGs, the player assume the role of a character (often in a fantasy world or science-fiction world) and takes control over many of that character's actions. MMORPGs are distinguished from single-player or small multi-player online RPGs by the number of players able to interact together, and by the game's persistent world (usually hosted by the game's publisher), which continues to exist and evolve while the player is offline and away from the game.

Although modern MMORPGs sometimes differ dramatically from their antecedents, many of them share some basic characteristics. These include several common features: persistent game environment, some form of progression, social interaction within the game, in-game culture, system architecture, membership in a group, and character customization.

www.ingramcontent.com/pod-product-compliance
Lightning Source LLC
LaVergne TN
LVHW060509170826